Where does the Sun go?

Written & Illustrated by Gary Craig

AN ELORA MEDIA BOOK

eloraMEDIA
expanding minds

Published in 2006 by Elora Media, LLC

Yelm, Washington

Text & Illustrations Copyright © Gary Craig 2004

The illustrations for this book were painted with acrylic watercolor and drawn in colored pencil.
The text was set in Garamond.

For information contact:

Elora Media, LLC

PMB 112, 1201 Yelm Avenue

Yelm, Washington 98597

www.eloramedia.com

Library of Congress Cataloging-in-Publication Data available.

Summary:

The delightful tale *Where Does the Sun Go?* is an adventure of the sun and its journey across the sky and over the earth.
Written in rhyming verse, this story is as amusing as it is educational, and will enchant preschoolers and early readers.

Printed and bound in the USA

ISBN 10-digit: 0-9786813-0-4

ISBN 13-digit: 978-0-9786813-0-2

To Harlow, Aspasia, and Laura
GC

It shines bright all day,

bathing all in its glow,

but when evening time comes,

where does the sun go?

When it crosses the sky

and then goes out of sight,

when the sky turns so dark,

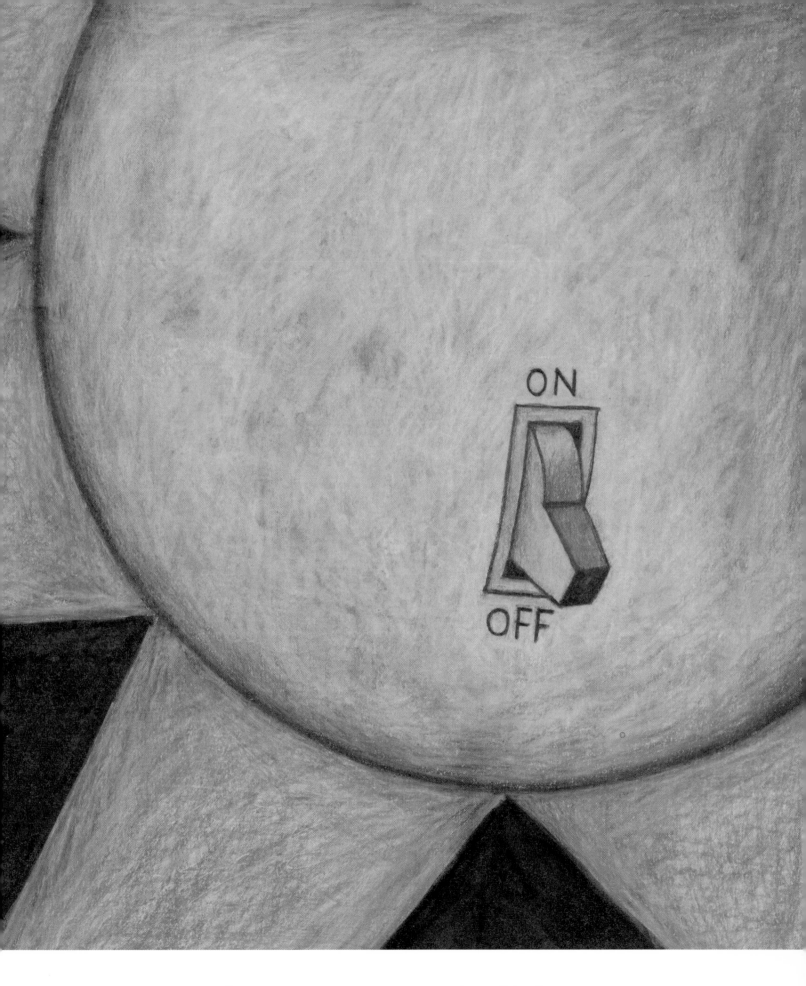

does it turn out its light?

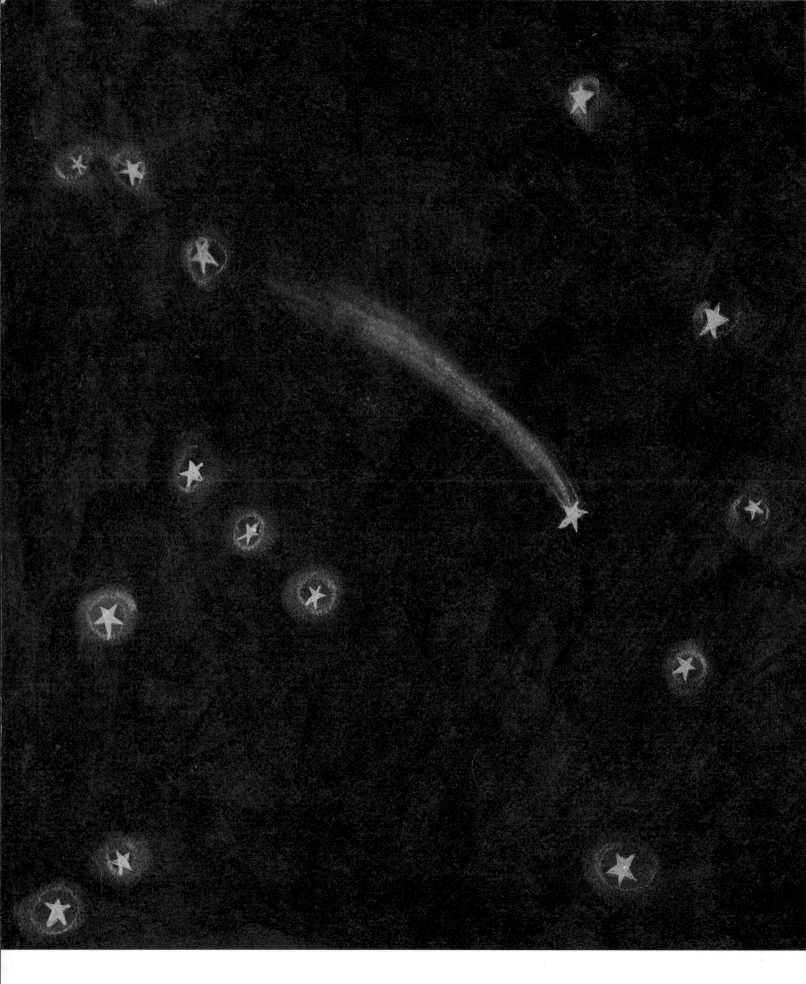

Just because all the stars

and the moon shine so bright

doesn't mean that the sun

has gone home for the night.

We all live on a ball called the Earth,

and it spins

and it circles the sun,

whose gold light never dims.

After being with us

for a glorious day,

the Earth spins like a top

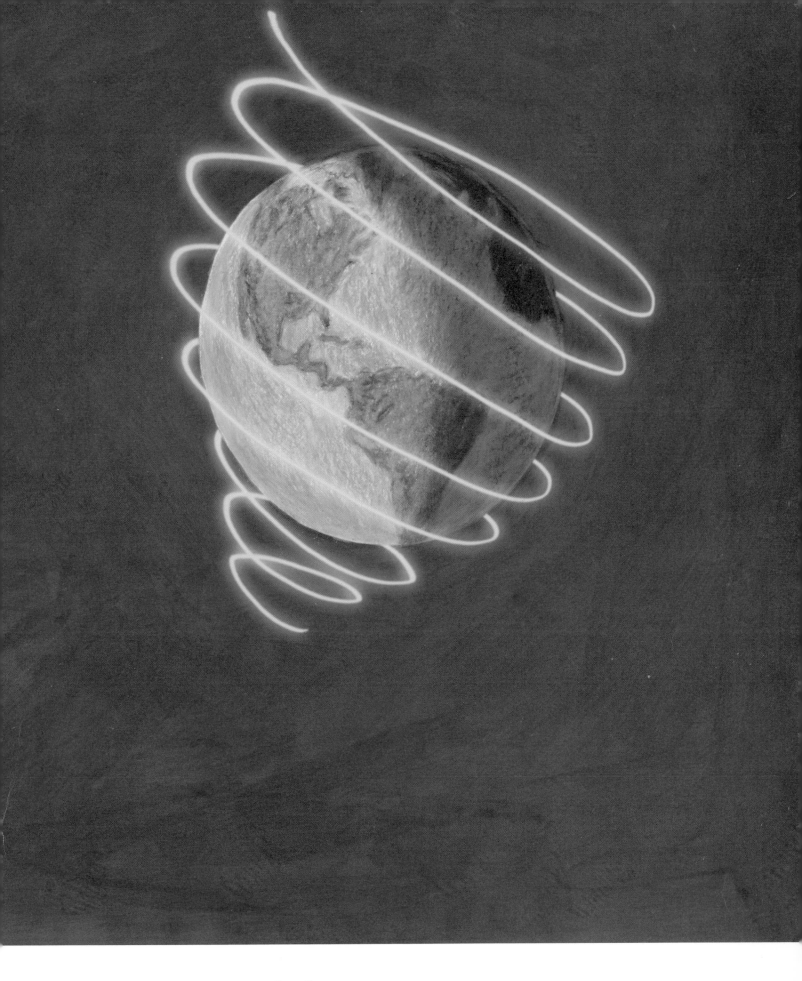

and the sun goes away.

On and on its rays shine when it leaves you and me,

and we spin off away and it's stars that we see.

Then the sun makes its way on all over the Earth,

and each country in turn feels its light and its mirth.

On to China and Russia

and Middle East sands,

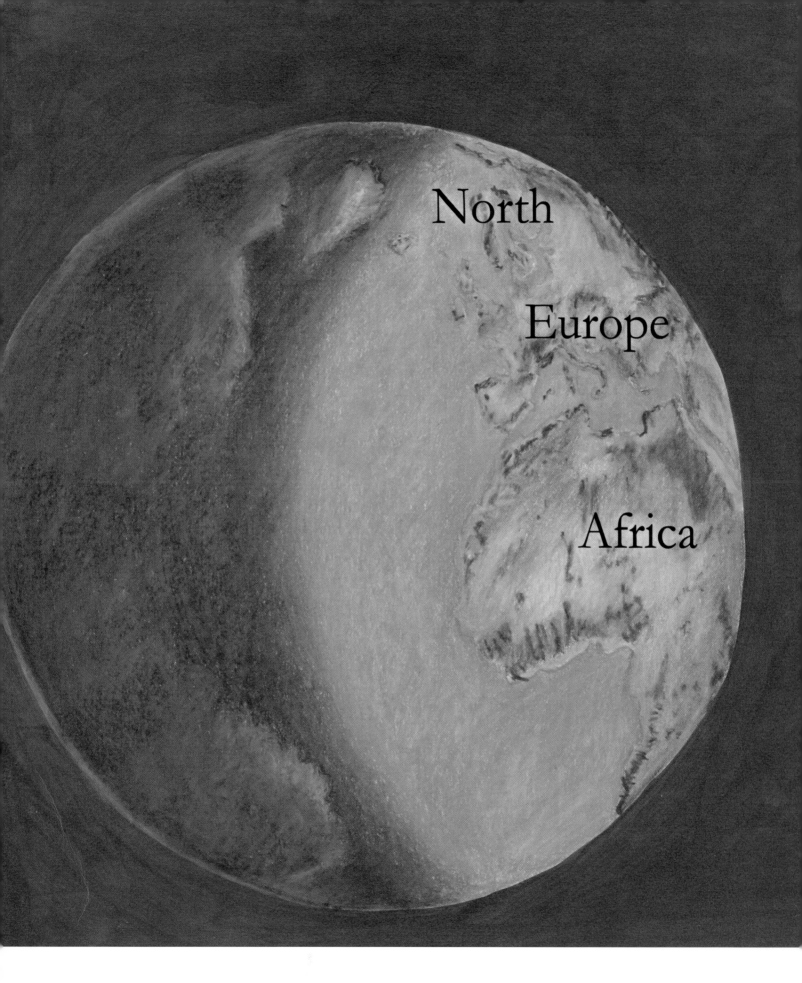

North

Europe

Africa

on to Africa, Europe,

and all northern lands.

And then after all this

it comes over the sea,

and returns once again

back to you and to me.

The End